WAITING ROOM

WAITING ROOM

Jennifer Zilm

BookThug / 2016

The production of this book was made possible through the generous assistance of the Canada Council for the Arts and the Ontario Arts Council. BookThug also acknowledges the support of the Government of Canada through the Canada Book Fund and the Government of Ontario through the Ontario Book Publishing Tax Credit and the Ontario Book Fund.

LIBRARY AND ARCHIVES CANADA
CATALOGUING IN PUBLICATION

Zilm, Jennifer, author
        Waiting room / Jennifer Zilm. – First edition.

Poems.
Issued in print and electronic formats.
ISBN 978-1-77166-214-7 (PAPERBACK)
ISBN 978-1-77166-215-4 (HTML)
ISBN 978-1-77166-216-1 (PDF)
ISBN 978-1-77166-217-8 (MOBI)

        I. Title.

PS8649.I52W53 2016   C811'.6   C2016-900591-7
                                     C2016-900592-5

PRINTED IN CANADA

for Graham and for all the doctors

CONTENTS

There is no refuge from listening to your own silence in the academy, in the pulpit, or in the safety of institutional bureaus and boards.

—Noah Eli Gordon, *The Source*

I. Sugar Discipline

LONG-LINED SONNET FOR DR. YOUNG

At the end of my benefits my mouth holds a temporary crown.
Along the Naugahyde arms of the tilted-back chair, my arms are
smooth and thick—the skin of an endangered African animal.
My iPod holds a slight density against the swell of bare belly,
cold beneath my T-shirt. One earphone is in, Eliot speaks with
the voice of the poet—St. Louis faking Queen's English—over
the buzzing insistence of the drill, latex fingers pulling at
my swollen, etherized gums: *these were the bones that were his eyes?*
The hygienist, middle-aged, Mexican, comments on the plasma screen
"the one hockey game I went to was Queen Elizabeth in her red dress,
dropping the—what do you call the rubber disk?—onto the ice."
Dr. Young, twenty-four and carving, ignores her. Beneath her breath
she remarks that beneath amalgams there is almost always decay.
Shaved calcium, dental cement, in my raised chair: I am enthroned.

REASONS YOU LOVE THE DENTIST

1. Your mouth straightjacketed
   you can finally stop
   talking.

2. You will be rewarded
   with paste and waxed paper
   for keeping still.

3. The drill is white noise: you
   creatively attend to silence.

4. A rush of water squirted into the
   lower bowl of your mouth
   reassures you: you won't ever be thirsty.

5. In the late 1980s, Dr. Killick patiently
   explained his sterilization techniques to your
   eight-year-old sister so she wouldn't fear
   contracting AIDS.

6. The chair is a classroom:
   you are privy to a new
   discourse, new words, old
   words reformed.

7. You are
   the centre of
   attention.

8. There are minerals in your mouth
   that you have never even considered.

9. Soon your swollen lips will thaw.
   Your gums will resurrect and your tongue
   will explore Dr. Young's architecture.

10. Now this hygienist
    whose Christian name you've forgotten
    acts as a pushy yoga instructor,
    forcing you to focus on breathing:
    through your nose, through your nose.

11. You grind your teeth,
    a war vet digs holes in your molars,
    carves crevices at the back of your incisors.
    Yet Dr. Young patiently rebuilds,
    adds height, matches shades of off-white
    and says that despite the grinding, the acid erosion,
    the slant of your bite, your damaged sibilants,
    you are "the most relaxed patient" she's ever had and

12. also you are lucky, you are still young
                                   you still have good bones.

MOUTH. GUARD.

Molded to the specifics of
your reconstructed mouth,
translucent, a ghost of
molar allowed for,
hypothetical mass of porcelain;
future implant or
bridge. Clasp it
over the half-moon,
bottom teeth.

Cripple your sibilants.

Go to bed.

II. Academy of Fragments

"Erase everything you have written,
but keep the notes in the margins."
—Osip Mandelstam

THE COMMITTEE MEETING

Jet-lagged, you say to the Doctors
who have gathered before you:
Whenever I stand to present
a paper I feel like a charlatan.
Your Swedish Doctor (associate)
bald with ginger stubble, responds:
I am afraid this noun is not part
of my English vocabulary.
Pop quiz: How many synonyms
can you think up in the next
twenty seconds? You say: *a faker.*
Suddenly there is scholarly consensus.
Your American Doctor (assistant)
clean-shaven with a Tyrolean chin
and the faint scent of a near-forgotten
stint at a Jerusalem Bible College, says:
There was a recent article about
this—peer reviewed—in the
Journal of Higher Education:
80% of academics feel the same way.
Your Head Doctor, the white-haired nun,
is outnumbered. Smiles ensue and satisfy.
It's never scholarship until statistics
are involved.

Freshly doctored, straight off the plane from a town in Indiana eponymous
    with a cathedral in France—
he is a Bachelor of Business Administration from an Ivy State and a Master
    of Theology from an Old Jerusalem Bible College. (Or is it BBA from
    Jerusalem Bible College and MTS from Ivy State? The chronology on the
    CV isn't clear).
Three times in one hour he says, *That's the best question I've heard all day.*
One time he even says it to you.

His attention is focused on uncovering the Semitic antecedents of the past
    participle used in the
Beatitudes. He has proven that Syriac manuscripts found in caves circling the
    Dead Sea convey the
word *blessed* as linguistically identical to the word *lucky.*

There are blue silk patches adhering to his elbows. He could have done
    anything with his life. He
could have managed a furniture warehouse in Michigan; pastored a
    predestined congregation of fourth
generation Dutch immigrants; he could have been the Governor of
    California—

but he *chose* to venture north to this Instro-University town to read Hebrew
    with you in the
basement seminar room, with the reproduction of Raphael's *Madonna and
    Child* above the white ornamental fireplace.

Blessings be.
You are so lucky.

FOOTNOTES TO THE ASSOCIATE PROFESSOR

He encourages[1] you to allow the footnote to overtake the page.[2]
He manages to be simultaneously bald, a redhead, and sexy.[3]
Post-Enlightenment, Postmodern:[4] He dialogues interfaith in his spare time.[5]
He digs through the bones of Galilean synagogues.[6]
His doctoral students always put male names in their dissertation titles.[7]

---

1   On your campus tour he shakes your hand the way
you always thought a man should shake a woman's hand:
firm, yet gentle, with the recognition of a mattered presence.
He laughs knowingly when you say, *Jesus must clearly have
been ginger.*

2   He writes your voice on the chalkboard in the main seminar room,
the one that isn't in the basement, the one displayed to guests,
to prospectives. You don't remember what you said, but perhaps it was
something about the elusive Messiah, about methods of excavating a parable.
You only recall his slender yet masculine hand
tracing white letters on the smooth, fecund green.

3   Once he is talking about whether to use the 3ʳᵈ person, the Royal We or the I in
scholarship, and as he says "subsequently" as 'sub-SEE-quently,' you immediately
begin to compose a letter to the OED to amend their pronunciation guide.

4   One of his research interests is Identity Formation. When they tear you apart
for using the words *mission* and *conversion* in the New Testament section of the
Canadian Society of Biblical Studies, he is at the back of the crowded lecture hall
and says nothing. Later, in an office in University Hall, he tells you that you are
absolutely right.

5   In that same aforementioned office, he says *You're interested in gender, aren't you?*
And you find yourself denying it, saying: *Not really. I'm not interested in anything.
Not anything.*

6   Later, in the basement, he tells you lovely things about your review of Jewish
archeology, and suggests you should publish your reading of footwashing in the
Gospel of John.

7   e.g., "Jesus the Galilean Exorcist"; "Matthew the Shepherd"; "Jesus: Restoration
Prophet"; "Luke the God-Fearer"; "Paul the Christ-Believer"; "Mark and the
Unveiled Temple"; "The Synoptic Joseph and the Fogged Window."

His Scandinavian children are all blonde.[8]

They are Church of Sweden agnostics. They sing Christmas hymns to the last surviving Swedish saint.[9]

---

8   Just before Christmas after your last seminar you gather with your "future colleagues" in his dense dining room adjacent to a jumbled book room to eat a "humble meal" of soup. You drink too much wine and argue after dinner with a burgeoning Gospel scholar about how to pronounce the word *trepidatious*.

9   For real. The saint's name is Lucy—
like the bones of the first human—
and she survived the Reformation.
The children wear paper leaf laurel halos
and sing to you in Swedish. His eyes
shine upon them; these are his most
beautiful footnotes, maybe, and his
two fair daughters sing like girls
raised by a man who knows how to
properly shake a woman's hand.

EMAIL TO THE FULL PROFESSOR

Subject: (no subject)
Date: (not specified)

Dear Dr. S,

I hope this email finds you.

Before our next appointment I wanted to mention
some thoughts I had in the hallway after my last meeting.
I was waiting for the Committee to calibrate the adequacy
of my progress, when you called me back
into your office to initial the form you would
then forward on to Graduate Studies.

You see, when I still thought I was a New Testament scholar,
I dreamed of a dissertation entitled *Saviour in the Sandbox:
a socio-material examination of Jesus and dirt.*
My primary sources would be the sight-giving miracles
in the gospels of Mark and John—Jesus pasting
mud and spit on a blind man's eyes—
and those verses where the judges bring an exposed woman
before the Messiah and he traces letters in the dust
rather than condemning her. I wanted to prove
this connects God forming Adam from feminine dirt
in the opening chapters of Genesis.

What I am trying to say is that I left the New Testament
because I realized that a PH.D wasn't going to teach me
what Jesus wrote on the ground in the orphan passage
appended to the fourth gospel. Also, those majuscule Greek letters
in the Early Witnesses looked so bold and oppressive.
But Hebrew, as you must know, is warm; the characters round

and open—an empty tomb we enter into.
Now that I have learned to write in script, my hand feels lovely
as I break the bottom line with my final *tzadehs*.

I can't provide a source, but I heard somewhere that
you ended up with some Hebrew fragments in your hands
when you were a young nun. You confessed
you wanted to make a grand point about music and prayer
but were contented, or rather overwhelmed, with those broken pieces
of paper in your feminine hands. Non-canonical
psalms. This is what always draws me back
to your research profile, despite the silences between us
in your office. I too would like to make a grand point
about angels and women and song and the Sonics of gendered prayer.
Yet I'm uncertain when you say I have to be careful
when defining *mysticism* and *transformation*.

Perhaps you're saying I shouldn't throw words around.
But listen: regarding your insistence that I completely revise
my chapter on the *Songs of the Sabbath
Sacrifice*: I can't go back to those vacant spaces.
It's not that I can't imagine what syllables filled them.
Once I start, I can't stop imagining everything else—
the second Jewish war, the flames, the taste of
boys in the back seat before I even learned the *Aleph
Bet,* the bones of that woman who died in childbirth
the archeologists dug up: a fetal skull trapped in the bones of her pelvis—
the question becomes not what could have been
in the disintegrated text, but what wasn't.
All the lines lost to ellipses, implied in brackets,
make me tremble like Jerusalem Syndrome crossed
with some repetition compulsion.

When I was in Jerusalem

I hired a cab at the Jaffa Gate in the Old City
on Shabbat to take me to the Dead Sea.
I saw only heaped rocks in those ruins.
So my tour guide and I walked away from the sign
that pointed to the dug out library and headed
toward the void in the cliff where a shepherd
first found those Judean mud pots.
Along they way we—Sharif and I—were distracted
by a small herd of gazelles. We approached them
slowly before their eyes unearthed us
(the Hebrew noun is *gazilim:* It is both masculine and plural).
The photo I took shows them scattering, letters
on a quickly decomposing canvas,
their bodies nearly indistinguishable
as they run back into the dust,
disappearing into the brackets of the hills.

DEAD SEA SCROLLS: A DISSERTATION ERASURE

ACKNOWLEDGMENTS

In the song circle,
unbroken, this image of
singing:
plain fashion, out of dust
everlasting, purified with
place
with the host of your
name.

AN EXTENDED DESCRIPTION OF DAUGHTERS

A daughter took on a heart—no longer
minded.
  She spoke in dialect, sending up
God with hymnic style.

  She spoke, inscribed

her garment in the thousands of their language.

PROCEDURE: I CALL "HUMAN CONTEXT."

The explicit degrees of how. This is

salient! Question literature about
the Dead. Women discussing this
disparity: these women's lives.

Practice: pay attention to re-reading.
Uncover in the caves all these
Fragmentary.

SOMETHING LIKE A PHRASE has been adopted
by Other. New herself, she notes
all their vivid ascents. Technical vocabulary
of Other picked up: the term communion

vis-à-vis human divide. She does
identify as the Qedushah: where
in the terms "Holy" and "Blessed"
following the Sacrifice cut off surpassing
holiness:

        the offering of tongue unsurpassable.
        Use this verse as evidence, become evident.

in the body of her, She opens
many voices
dropped, the veil removed
in some Cave.

ANGELOMORPHISM: THE SHIFTED CENTRE

A departure from all anthropology.

All the implications of attempted, ancient,
encroaching these sites of worship.

The universe in microcosm a book
regaining the roots found in image.
A cult statue: a god saying

"humanity breathing is the root of
the locus of the divine presence."

AN OBVIOUS PROBLEM FOR READING IS LAMENTING:

A crucial part of a gulf
between this passage and imagination.

These garments the only artifact of
Still available.

    The main purpose of
worship can be summarized: pristine
access / possible proximity / also conformity

to character. Mode of thinking
continues in theology of lost.

Even basic antiquity.

It   is   impossible   to   read   unpersuaded
by the novelty of reading!

Many   read   the   inkling   as   innovation:
interested   in   the   reference   to   a   body,

the   corpus.   The   most   important   of   these
is   the   *Related:*   discussing   a   point
in   the   salient   experiential,

reflecting a transcendent presence,
which stands visible.

                                        Material   leads   to
longing   for   closer   relationship   with
this   bewildering.

THIS "WORKING DEFINITION"

Controversial, the morass perhaps
inspired to elude scholarly definition.

Acknowledges a transcendent
visible world, uncontroversial.

Any definition is anthropology,
authors humanity, judgments
about the existence of something.

Therefore exclude scholarly investigation
altogether.

Highlighting their worship as trans-
formed lucid, isolate a microcosm
of a preliminary understanding
of differing.

The conductor's score a weekly cultic drama.
The cast—angels, human participants—
the roles of these a process of Songs subsumed.

The discourse made salient. Notes in Songs:
the past undeniable.

As notes reflect a common current, keenly.

Within the corpus found One Fragmentary,
in the liturgical world. Witness—unattested—to reading
wife backwards: creeping, retelling.
Prelapsarian manuscripts contain a female Fragmentary.
In prayer, passive, merely participating,
following pages, pay attention to titles and pronouns.

Who speaks in the liturgy? To get a sense of preserved fragments:
pay attention.

This is an imposed break inherent in the *However.*
Grasp the material:

to bear seed h]oly one, Daughter of Truth, darling.
She has the midst, fragments. The crux of the wedding
wholly reconstructed. We have holy ones syntactically
proximate to singular giving.

We find a Daughter of Truth who walks and then   breaks. The opening
of the line is missing, female companion   in the midst of breaks—   broken

Daughter of Truth—companion, wife—all re
constructed. The Reconstructed, the prim-
eval fragment of jubilees, form of tempting
performance related to expulsion.

                             One of the Preferred is unparalleled.
Daughter of Truth warrants translating. Trans-
lating, the Daughter of Truth intertextually led
to a garment of exalted overflowing.

The Daughter of Truth in *this* mystery, Fragmentary,
a bride possessing.

The Daughter of Truth is
considering this, and linking a sense
of what being a Daughter may entail.

Clothed in elaborating the verb boundless,
a verbal divine presence. Prayer
in the Sectarian Possible. Here

we relate the Daughter of Truth
truly, and it is not enough, just
to say this. Conceptually
the same sphere, within the liturgical
discourse of this text at least,
the Daughter of Truth has a role to play.

She is angels, in a shared space, in fragments,
interrelated, outlined subtly. Here:
this is marriage of veil and testimony
in the veil; the veil for you the holy
place from the most holy place.

The Daughter of Truth privileges We,
use of presence, of However

the space   broken

BIBLIOPHAGE: AN ESSAY

Let's not drop names
but let the reader
remember
a Persian poet murder
dreaming, suffusing
the lungs of a codex
in river water. A prophet
chewing the flesh of his
page, swallowing up
the α. A revelator
copy-call killing,
chewing down to the ω.
Moses chucking tablets
against a desert floor
and watching them
shatter. The owners of
the city's oldest bookstore
discovering their
remainders before
throwing them out.

When does torture stop short of murder? What is
the difference between that poet, that prophet, that bookstore, that revelator
and the crowds at Nuremburg and Alexandria and their hot textual genocide?
Sometimes you think of Sylvia Plath tearing into the pages of Ted Hughes'
Collected Works of William Shakespeare and it reminds you of the whole healthy
scent of burning leaves in a suburban park when you were eight years old. It
makes you think of lust. The prophets say the taste of text is sweet and bitter.
Sugar discipline. The sweet is the ink and the bitter is the paper. A child learns
the alphabet in honey. Watch the carnal way in which you underline your
favourite stanza. That violation; bruising marginalia. Last night I dreamed the
ghosts of the librarians of Alexandria came to me and said:

Now as then it is the flames we remember.
Warm winter, that textual autumn.
The abundant scent of smouldering papyrus.
All the words we never read and how we
always washed our hands before we touched
those scrolls. Alexandria, winter
behind crumbling stones, leaves burning.
The hands casting text into fire, a touch
we envied. The expanding void of all
the lines our fingers our tongue had never traced.

CATACOMBS

You said:
If these pictures are so damn holy,
how come the paint wears away?

You fingered the spot on the wall where Mother Mary's skirt was missing.
You were still bummed by the misleading directions in the guidebook and
how the bus driver had pretended not to understand when you asked him in
Italian. You'd been enrolled in that Continuing Ed. class for six weeks and had
only missed half the classes. You were also smarting because the driver spoke
of you to another passenger, laughed lightly, said the word
Americano.

The Italy you wanted was not
two-dimensional.

You wanted hulking marble statues and starch; red wine and women in
blue dresses with large, white polka dots, women who ride on the backs of
scooters and let their dresses blow up over round, brown thighs; or women
who pedal bikes with baguettes in their baskets, wearing high-heeled sandals
that expose red toenails. I am certain you saw haphazard dark hair falling
over arched cheeks. I suppose you were picturing a wide, well-lit city square
when you asked me why we would waste a day in a suburban graveyard.

I said:
Maybe God isn't an archivist
trying to be quick-witted.

But I knew 'archivist' was not the word I wanted. I wanted a word that means
someone whose job it is to preserve old paint. But I didn't know that word
and you looked at me in a way that implied that you knew exactly what it
was, that you could spell it with your eyes closed, not even needing to trace
the letters with your finger in the air.

Still, I was glad it was cool
underground.

I wore sneakers with thick arches that made my feet itch.
I also wore a light sweater because I heard you had to cover your arms in
holy places. Under my T-shirt the money belt holding our passports and
guidebook chaffed against my bare skin.

III. Singular Room Occupancy:
Cantos from Main & Hastings

For Kyla (1980–2013)

JOB DESCRIPTION:

working with
dually diagnosed
"hard to house"
adults, the project
worker is primarily
called upon to use
empathy and boundaries
to creatively meet
the day-to-day
needs of the residents[10]

---

10 (in accordance with Canadian Union of Public Employees, equal opportunity
   employer, etc., etc.)

FIELD TRIP, ALMOST THE WEST SIDE

Sometimes winter   rains   you notice
          gladly the sheets   a safety
of baby blue   umbrella   like lived art
          in faux leather   boots
high-buttoned   duffle coat   secretly grateful
          for wet   gentrified
pavement   rejuvenated   neon signs.

                    Mount Pleasant. *SoMa*.

This   other   country, this

          exotic

                    neighbourhood.

Remember October?   How you thought   the East   extended   past
Columbia   —that boundary—   past   Victory Square   trickling bodies
West End   sprinkling   beggars
          liberally   as pepper
spare change   hand-written signs
dandelion   of ghetto   blowing
          ghostly   globe
throughout

          the city's core.

Yet the rain in *this* neighbourhood
is white noise; you can pretend
it isn't even East Vancouver.
Open the door to the Cottage
Bistro and find your seat

Beneath   a hand-painted   sign, inside
       a poet   reads
a *Still Life*   dedicated   to everyone
      suffering   addiction
depression   self-loathing   it's obvious,
      despite   tinsel
low lights   melted   goat cheese
      red wine   drifting
through   genuine   gentle
      applause   the poem
isn't enough   to go   around
      they aren't   here
to receive   this   unrapt
      gift   you
lose   the poem   in the
      dedication   you
back   through   the back
      door.

WOMEN'S RESIDENTIAL RECOVERY

From the shore canto one

Now, from the intersection, let
poetry wake again. Calliope

strain   colour   unclouded
Vancouver   blue echo   Vancouver blue

sea   to   sky.

My newed eyes.

                                              How To:
Rip My Eyes   **Away.**

Jodi flails, a mixture of up and down in her blood.
Before her detox intake, her body is taught—

*If I'm going to be locked up for ten days
I need to dunk myself in the ocean.*

North from the crux , you follow her
to the Secret of the City beach,
a skyline present yet remote.
She is tanned, her hair is dirty,
she is missing teeth, and laughing

you place   a single   toe into the   ocean, skin
rimming   a red   painted nail   corroded pink
by autumn   water

In the cab from Ocean Road to Van Detox she freewheels
her own DSM, nine circles of recovery symptoms.

Fuck lithium. Fuck Epival.
Mood stabilizers are such bullshit.
I have trained every worker in this 'hood.
Social-working; outreaching.
When I get out, I'll teach you
HOW TO: Jaywalk the Right Way.
I have ten minutes until my intake
just let me wait here
in the garden

On the way home: the confrontation of Main and Hastings, again.
Outside Owl Pharmacy, a drunk interrogates you: "*Studento?*
Studento?" A hand reaches to grasp the edge of your denim jacket.
Then, home: You lie beneath two comforters. One for spring,
the other for winter, even though it is only *fall*. You splurge,
read bloodroot, a translated *lingua franca:* your violent need for words.

HALLWAY, RAINIER HOTEL RESIDENTIAL
WOMEN'S RECOVERY PROGRAM, AN ELEGY

rectangle round the kitchen   mine eyes endured

police consolation   some unknown thing

whatever happened you did the right thing

a body in a room/square footage of
a heart/o Shades/a brief space
I turned/a renovated logging hotel/
housing women/held in check/
Resurrection of a neon sign:

Amazement written in my eyes, I think,
in changing colours for the Shade withdrew
Smiling(?) and I
plunged forward/after

(how many languages
can translate a pronoun)

Elle sie she   lei

                              eccola

how to girl the second person
in our language without
brackets:

                    You (feminine singular)
I will never breathe this fast again

JOURNALING

Now let us perform a new-age gerund
O wrecked ladies of this white-less winter,
in our cold, borrowed common room, wracked by the rain

in this light from three walls of windows, a homemade
quilt nailed to the fourth, west-facing. Let us now
cultivate silence and ignore the sounds of trolley busses

on Cordova, their wheezing punctured by
snaps of electric friction that has them chained
to the road by wires. There is too much

light, too much light. Attend with your pencils
and pretty, gifted books. Recovery: You
(*feminine singular*). It's your turn. O freckled

blonde, your half-closed eyes, pupils pinned in blue,
frozen, tell us your PTSD lucid dream unknowing.
Speak to us of Alexandria!

> *I had a dream we were brought here by ships.*
> *I don't know about Adam and Eve, but*
> *I heard all the old books were lost in fire...*
>
> *I wanted to live beside the beach*
> *but I swear the vapours make it colder*
> *than On-Terrible. There is a shelter*
>
> *further down Cordova that says their doors*
> *are always open to women. But I*
> *am going to recover in one of those*

treatment houses in the Valley—Look out!
Child on the Block!—Tangled, I fell. My
veins (when I can find them) make puddles on

the floor. There where my name is lost, I came
hitchhiking. My sputtered blood. There is one
place where there are no windows, so I feel

safe. One of the Houses in the Valley
is called The River. The other the Wave Pool:
Welcome Home. But you work there

—sweat equity—and it's hard to get
into: I got rejected because I
was pregnant, but I'm not pregnant any-

more but for now, I'm just working my own
program. Step 2 is I am powerless
against and I have a power, higher.

See, I have journal'd an inventory—
accepting what I cannot change—I am
just penitent, pardoned, strong with wanting.

WITNESSED INGESTION

Short shifts mostly/12 hours a day.
Funding cuts/basic wound care.

Your client

 tells you a joke as she swallows
 her methadone. Two gulps, a blue prison tat
 on her wrist exposed
 when she hands back
 the brown plastic. You black out

the name. Your client's

 quotidian is 12 shots
 of vodka to maintain.
 His favourite food is pickles.
 His meals are free, but he feeds them to a fat
 seagull in your country's poorest postal code.

The category casual does not work.
The category casual does not work.

Auxiliary seems apt. Your helpless
sense of a grateful periphery.

You say: *Early in my career I made a composite of countless characters
supplicating to a bus driver, seeking a free ride to Strathcona mental health.*

Now you bring your pay stub to a bank.
In the box provided for occupation
on your mortgage application
you write *Witness.*

SAFE: INJECTION SITE

Intro. harm reduction: purity & danger[11]

Prerequisites may include, but are not
limited to a needle stick, a hand
in a puddle of Hep C blood, the words
hidden in the acronyms HIV and
ARV, and perhaps C Defficle (As
one of your classmates is about
to undergo a *cum laude* project to get a
fecal transplant, his shit being infected.)

Project One: "Discount." The body of a man,
barefoot; a hot spiced-vinegar smell that echoes
throughout the waiting room. Not flailing,
but dancing. He jumps, the crisp fluorescent
feathers of a Halloween boa encircle his neck.
Glistening pink wounds on his cheeks,
his left hand runs a safety razor
over an uneven crew cut. The student
will remain undistracted by his smile—
an incisor missing—wabi-sabi grin.
The student will move to his shopping cart
and extract the dirty rigs one by one—the dregs
of someone's blood and hints of mystery dope inter-
mingled. Use tongs and baby-blue exam-gloved
hands. Place the rigs into yellow plastic:
a haz-mat bucket. When he finds
them missing, he will shout and then forgive:
the student will successfully let
his/herself be chastised/forgiven.
(Let him grant you something.)

---

11 Prerequisites may also include a *Bachelor of Arts, a Bachelor of Social Work, or the
approximate equivalent of education and experience.*

Project Two: In the injection room.
He will say *I need help.* The student will map
her own veins and model her mapping fingers
over the scar tissue—again with latex
fingertips. Then find the standing vein, tie a
loose knot with azure rubber, let the blood
concentrate. Stand back and watch this
incision. Do not transfix eyes as
the blood floods upward into the syringe.
Push the blood and speed into the vein:
swiftly unleash the ersatz tourniquet
(he will shake his head, slap his face,
his brown eyes will blink to hold it all in).

    The student will—

MATH LESSON: INSITE FRONT DESK

I know the density of gravity,
  he says in the waiting room

                                        I know

the density of the planet—

                                        what is the math thing

you learn in high school?

$(\sin^2\theta + \cos^2\theta = 1)$?[12]

                                        Not trigonometry,[13]

$$\Delta t^{l} = \frac{\Delta t}{\sqrt{1 - \frac{v^2}{c^2}}} \quad ?[14]$$

not physics,

                                        not geometry—[15]

---

12 Where θ is any angle.
13 From the Greek: to measure triangulation.
14 Where Δt is the time that passes according to a stationary observer; Δt^{l} is the time
   that passes according to an observer in motion.
15 From the Greek: to measure the earth.

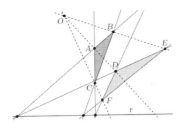

that's just

drawing

—ALGEBRA—[16]

$(a - B - C - \Delta - \theta = x)$

I know what X is

don't know how I know but I know

---

16 From the Arabic: to put fragments back together.

CHEMISTRY

Up; see also: Powder
Down; see also: Heroin
—Speedball (*v./n.*) together

Sideways; see also: Gak; see also: Gib; see also: Speed

(this
        recipe you can
never grasp)
(everyday a new synonym)

Goofball (*v./n.*) Sideways with Down.

Concentrated Up = Rock. You can melt Up
        in your tiny tin beaker with Vitamin C

a flame held inches from your fingers.

ART HISTORY: HOW THE CEILING LOOKS FROM OUTSIDE

On Hastings as far west as Dunsmuir, with his shopping cart:

I don't know why men have to hit women I don't know why women have to kill
  their babies I don't know why
sometimes it seems that
man is biting the hand that created him

There is a Chihuahua on a scaffold nipping
            at that painting of God
and his extended fingers

in that church
                    in Italy.

RIFF ON CANTO SIX

(BRAZEN ERASURE ON THE BUNDAY BINNER'S MARKET)

I was in the crowd that day. Markets make me nervous.
So many deferred problems, all the promises to buy.
Remember the way merchants hemmed me in the old city?

Hey beautiful
hey pretty eyes
it doesn't cost anything to smile

My face is thrown back
at me everywhere.

The hunchback on the corner has had her hair cut again.
Close crop. Dirty seagull. Drug debts.
Sometimes it grows long and surprises me—so shiny.

I like that little hunchback.
She's cute I hope she doesn't die
like Selma died like John died like that other one died
don't worry so much about it you'll live longer and get a tax rebate

Before break I was dealing with The Other Public.
Front desk. This hotel of grief. No, we don't have
rooms to rent to you, Public. This is *Housing*.
These are people living in a gerund.

Let judgment suspend.
Be it strange and manifest:
the tremble possesses a lingering.

We are all participles. We are all gerunds.

The sweat in the garden, an empire of waste, that which saved the sacred green space beside the safe injection site and the gated rubble between the Regent Hotel and Brandiz Pub. Bible verse, Genesis, spray-painted on plywood border: *the nephilm are on the earth in these days.*

How do you spell neighbourhood? My autocorrect is fucking up I need
to get one of those new Blackberries how do you spell
neighbourhood? As in: I've got to get out of this
neighbourhood—

brazen erasure on the Sunday Binner's Market:
The hazard tried to catch me anon
pushes through, remembers away
in that crowd, that day
                    turning
everywhere my face bought outstretched flesh.

She. Her. Procure her. Grow holy. Speed think condemn.
           All these people.
Fully clear to me this con. Flash the payment. Debt deep
waters reject she 'twixt smiling and tired
veils the facts. Speedy reach.
Head upon eyes watching
eyed the ascent. My self-absorbed Sullen.
The shade-embraced Other.
O house o Bond Mistress swift.
City's name: One Wall/Devour Wretched.
Thy seas, coasts read her:

you snatched at her. This wild judgment
strange and manifest: Thou lingering
this garden of waste.

Come. See. Thy persecuted sore, wounds

come heart of thy city, widowed.
Come, slain aloof
plan our eyes swarming.

Be glad
        arts urbane

                whose planning so

        redesigned

                                a woman sick

                softest, turning

ELEGY, A RAIN FRAGMENT

The rain a silk mesh blanket,
giddy at a prose poem, a monologue
of hobos, a tiny leaf
a prayer of thresholds. *Theft under*
your chargeable offense, your diagnosis. *Goodbye*
from the boundary shore. If she said
that to me

IV. This Holy Room/the great listeners

Talking therapies come out of psychoanalysis, which in turn comes out of the ritual disclosure of dangerous thoughts first formalized in the church confessional.

—Andrew Solomon,
The Noonday Demon

DIAGNOSES

Your autobiography, on tinfoil,
in aquamarine ink. Diagnosis subtle.
Answer this multiple-choice question:
Do you grab objects from other people?

ADD: Does your brain loop pictures
of your mouth kissing the mouth of a lanky Arab
cab driver and do you run your palms over door knobs
eight times and wash your hands with bleach & sunlight?

OCD: Do you lose your edges and
the boundaries between your body
and another body and the pavement
and the deep blue sea?

BORDERLINE: (Axis II). Historians say
Orpheus was Borderline with OCD features—
that's why he couldn't stop turning around.
Lot's wife too—

SALINITY: a side effect of the some
of the best medications. Also

SKIN RASH: only on the inside
of your hands. But still the medication is a

MIRACLE: its touch is jellyfish/devilfish
velvet walking the shine of your brain

YOUR HEART: its polished surface.

CLEAN.

SEVEN SEEING PARTS FOR DR. BARNHOUSE

1.

Once she wrote of you in her notebook:
There is nothing I can do that would make her
withhold her listening. Dr. Barnhouse, you forgot
about her dream of being trapped in the subway tunnel
en route to her appointment, blue sparks heading
for her eyes. She swears she told you.
"Shock" treatment is like sleep, you said.
Reassuring sibilance: *I swear*
I will be with you the whole time.

Religious fanatics deep in your childhood, a failed early marriage—
you initially blessed her trip to England:
I was bending over backwards not to take a piece of her.
Crescent spectacles on the bridge of your nose,
you signed a permission slip, a love letter, an R$_x$: *Love, Ruth.*
If I save only you my practice makes perfect.

2.

Her session notes are at last in the un-expunged journals.
Thirty years hidden but not burned.
What they reveal: *"I hate hate*
hate… thank you, Doctor, I sure do hate…" How she cried only
in the hidden corner of your office: you listened.

3.

Dr. Barnhouse, you likely gave Sylvia
an extra six to ten years.
when she first entered into your
therapeutic presence you were as
young as she was at her death:

                                                  that blattered teenager.
                      A novice,
when she told you about the machine, the cerulean jolts, you became
as still as voice not speaking.
                   Then: *She set something on my tongue;*
darkness obliterated me like white on a chalkboard.

                                           The soothing
black and silence. You with her the whole time. That communion.
An open-eyed doctor and a sleep-zapped *Mädchen*, two girl bodies
together in the tunnel.

4.

I wanted her away from them, you said.

5.

As an old lady in a well-ordered apartment
full of records and books, you ceased listening
to classical music and read only mystery novels.

I can't imagine it's worth that much, you said before
you sold your copy of *The Colossus* inscribed *With Love.*
I don't need it: she is in my heart. You held your hands
a foot apart to indicate the volume of her last letters.
You burnt each one. *I tried to*

                                        bring her back.

With the proceeds of your book sale, you
purchased tickets for an Alaskan cruise,
a cardiac dilation, hidden, ascending within you.

6.

Most intact aortic aneurysms do not produce symptoms
yet at the end of the last century, you suspected.
Another physician confirmed your diagnosis.
A second opinion. You could not bear
walking life as a time bomb; you went beneath
the knife instead of sailing to Alaska.
Your kidneys broke down: the surgeon
saved your heart for naught.

7.

We live out the parts of ourselves that aren't patients
in (y)our blind spots;
dog whistle a dance in your tone deafness.

                              O great unseeing; O vast
withheld listening.

'WHAT A QUEER THING TOUCH IS'

Therapeutic Notes of V. van Gogh and M. Peyron

1. EPISTLE TO THEO

I prescribed him a portrait. The retinue
in his tiny black eyes, the questions
he evades with sudden answers,
the vague and veiled secrets
in his moustache.

His wife doesn't believe I am ill.
If she is willing to sit I will paint
that dusty slash of grass, her faded
insignificant face.

Yesterday I dropped my duplication
of the *Piéta* in oil and have
begun to recapture it from memory.

M. Peyron is kind, indulgent—
he has permitted this liberty:
to work, mostly undisturbed,
in the makeshift studio edging
the sanitarium.

When you speak to him,
his voice will tell you
myriad things. If he is precise
believe none of it.

I fear the patient, the ginger Dutchman, has too much
      religion in his brain, he spent a sojourn painting
           the grey wives of miners and preaching the Gospel.
                 Yet he refused to learn Latin, so I fear his religion
                       is most uninformed, most delusional.
                           Yesterday in the midst of his ravings
                              at the easel, he "preached" a passage
                                 he swears is found in the scripture,
                                 where Christ took his time restoring
                                     the sight of a blind man:

          "First he touched and said, 'What do you see?'
        The blind man answered that he saw trees walking
       like men. Then the savior dirtied his hands with earwax,
     spittle and mud and applied his fingers to the eyes of the half-
    blind man just as I am now applying ochre oil to my canvas
  to reveal the wheat fields.

Ochre in his eyes, the now-seeing man saw
  completely. All this is just to say that one must accustom one's eyes slowly

        to a different light."

Patient reports his only symptoms as "this dizziness" and "the idleness of the
south," and that he has recently dropped some portrait of Our Lady into oil,
damaging it beyond recognition. One does not expect a madman, however,
to recognize his delusions as such.
                             Now for the weekend,
     I shall put his religious sickness
   out of my mind,
             and take my wife to Lourdes.

DR. GACHET'S WALK

1. THE DAY OF VINCENT'S DEATH

Dr. Gachet was first with a bouquet
of sunflowers, of which Vincent was so
fond. "If you walk along the river from
Auvers-sur-Oise to Pontoise, you can breathe
many of Pissarro's vistas. I think
I'll take that walk today," the doctor tells
Theo, his hands now devoid of blossoms.
It is such a gift, he thinks, to be seen
by a patient in oils. My thesis
Étude sur la Mélancolie restrained
vibrant in blue, black, with just a hint of
yellow, my elbow on a closed book, fist
pushing my cheek into my listening
face, but my blue away eyes, he captured
my distraction: his session, his seeing.

2. MEMORY: THE FIRST SESSION

Why don't we have our first appointment
in the room where I do my paintings.
I know the light is poor from the tiny windows
and there is no lock to stop the children
from bursting in occasionally, but there
are peacocks in the backyard and I knew
Cezanne personally.
Vincent diagnosed: this country doctor   is in worse shape
                                             than I am,
                                             perhaps he can help me.

3. DR. PAUL GACHET, CV

Education

- Bachelor of Arts from the University of Paris
- In-depth study of the obstetrics of the asylum at Bicêtre, almost a century before Foucault
- Completed a sub-specialty in the disease of *Melancholia* (1885) under the supervision of the great Armond Trousseau

Interests and Hobbies

- Painting

Notable Career Highlights

- Prescribed supplemental milk to children, when such a prescription was still novel
- Extensive impressionistic experience
- Saw Renoir through pneumonia, advised him not to sever his leg (he didn't listen, but a doctor can't be responsible for every outcome)
- Cared for Vincent from May–July 1890. Six Weeks.
- Told him I would gladly trade places with him. Asked him to call me "Paul"

4. COLOUR THERAPY

Now, on Pissarro's walk, the light attack of summer. Suddenly
blunted green hills, the dust of the once-yellow road now beige.
Dr. Gachet, you are thinking maybe of the colours
that compose melancholia. *The veiled lights of the North,*
the clouded prism of sky. Seeing red, the fast
break of dread, the way hands seek to touch a corner of gold.
The whole and broken yellows, Vincent said, *the great cathedral*
gives me the blues. His diagnosis always flowing
from his fingers to the brush to create your eyes.

SPIRITUAL MEDIA

1. DIRECTIVES: FOLLOW THIS POEM

@ShoppersDrugMart
                    pharmacists as primary care
            #yourlifestore #youregonnabehappy

@VCHhealthcare
                urban physicians and their

                                    atrophied skills

        #carepointclinic

@seroquelXR05 antipsychotics—even in sub-therapeutic doses—
can stop your period
#mypsychiatristsaysihaveexcellentboundaries

2. HISTOIRE DU LIVRE

Everyone you've ever known seems a monotheist,
eyes entranced by this dynamic book.

                      And you,
I have no way of knowing the moment
you enter the presence of my
pixelated freckles.

How much of this conversation
                is palimpsest, cut and paste?

          How do I read
your pauses? If you
juxtapose a link into our chat
and my clicking fingers open music,
how can I be certain you are
                singing to me?

Oh my, it's too obvious to be stated, isn't it?
Anti-social media.

Everyone on the bus skirting Hastings tilts their head downward
toward some hand-held light, all ears plugged by bits of black plastic.
But unplugged you still notice no one, only that the snow changes shape
here, and refuses to be named. Rain is too solid, sleet too wet, you barely
glimpse the neo-gothic legacy of Andrew Carnegie, the public library,
the R_x street market: you try to remember where you heard that
Zopiclone=Imovane, that heroin is both *soft* and *down*.

At the crossroads of the #4, the drivers switch places,
and the passenger beside you demands your pause
for his question, black and metal teeth,
breath of tobacco, Listerine, laughing when you insist
you don't understand his 20th-century Mandarin.

You focus on your destination. Westside, a windowless office
to change your core beliefs with alternating pulses of sound.
Where you feel the trauma up from your stomach, twitter
of a long ago memory, linked in to 1990s foam headphones,

she—MSW, RCC, carved Haida silver earrings—offering only
her heyschastic whisper

  good, good...

Praising you for holding still on a floral couch,
with your eyes closed, listening.

PLACING THE FRAGMENTS: INSTRUCTIONS FOR GRIEVING AN UNFINISHED DISSERTATION

sur le papyrus écrite: האישההודות
a) the woman, thanksgivings
b) the man of thanksgiving

1.

You are to enter a therapist's office.

Note there is no window,
that a century plant is blooming
beneath the concentrated light
of a desk lamp, a calendar
lists a statistical koan measuring
the ingredients for genius:
three-quarters' cup perspiration,
one-quarter cup inspiration.

Note there are two chairs
for you to choose from. One is *Ikea*—
will tilt you back, approximates
the vulnerability of a sofa—
the other will put you eye to eye
with your confessor.

Chose neither.

Place your knees on the short
carpeted floor. Unwrap
150 pages of double-spaced text
and spread them before you.

Fold your torso forward.[17]

(Two weeks of hours have led you to this
prostration, this splash of leaked mascara
onto Xeroxed paper, against your face
as though it was tissue soft. Your puckered
lips say a silent prayer, an eye opens onto

    "the liturgical discourse of this text,
      at least")

Accept these as your fragments.
If you are very lucky, some day
a shepherd may light upon them;
an archaeologist may speculate
upon your unwritten ending.

---

17 In 1947 some Bedouin shepherds
entered a cave in Judea and uncovered
some unadorned clay jars brimming
with broken paper. "The most important
archaeological discovery of the 20th century."
It was really only handwriting
on the refined skins of kosher animals:
cow, calf, sheep, goat and gazelle.
The shepherds brought the paper
to East Jerusalem, and the paper
drove archaeologists to the desert.
They raced into more caves, and in turn,
the shepherds, outmanoeuvring
the archaeologists, peddled treasure maps,
producing jar after jar of handwriting
that in turn produced a thousand dissertations
that flooded the academic black market.

Dr. Luria is a 16th-century Kabbalist.
Dr. Luria is *not* a 16th-century Kabbalist?
Dr. Luria is a neuropsychologist, Dr. Luria
writes S

      Synaesthete S senses a world
in each word of a poem, an addiction
to narrative, association

and I-not S-trying
with Benzo brain memory suppressant
to just listen to sound, stop sculpting story
just read the R$_x$ enunciate

Zopi CLONE (electric sheep, robots with memory)

PRN: GABA pent in (0 contain my chatter)
Te MAZE pam (squared, running in circles)
seroquel/quetiapine (shh shh) HS

        h
         S

MY PSYCHIATRIST WAS A MATH MAJOR

Percentage of people who won't ever like me: 30%
Percentage of people who will suffer from depression in their lifetime: 25%
Percentage of patients for whom antidepressants will be efficacious: 20%
Percentage of patients for whom antidepressants will act only as placebo: 80%

Do you remember when I told you about
that phone call to my father to ask about
Bach? There was a memory of baroque guitar
at a campsite, a fear of the campfire,
of being all together in a tent. I
wanted to understand what happened: why
music and forest together still cause my hands to
tremor. My father spoke about point/counter-
point, why it was so fascinating. You
diagnosed this as a meaningful father/daughter
exchange; you inquired about symptoms, used
percentages. How can you help me?

Consider a three-year study that compared
Paroxetine 40 mg/OD with Clonazepam 2 mg/OD (HS)
that demonstrated subjects on Clonazepam
had better outcomes vis-à-vis panic disorder.[18]
There were concerns about destroying the patients'
sleep architecture. Further, pharmaceutical
treatment should be complemented by cognitive/
behavioural therapy (200 ml) and exercise/
lifestyle (300 ml) and an equal mix of mindfulness and
combat breathing (sprinkle liberally to taste).

---

18 Panic disorder here denotes
that hard breath in the subject's chest
and the quiver in his/her bowels.

Dr. K, my eye has always been drawn to
the top of your bookshelf. In our windowless
holy room, there is a copy of *Karamazov* and your
paperback copy of *The Castle,* a print of a blue loon
laying eggs, watercolor weeds on white paper.
Once in the late minutes of our dense therapeutic
hour, you told me the image came with the office,
but the crayoned paper taped to its frame—
a five-year-old's *Supernova,* was your own.
Then you wrote a sacred script, a list poem R_x
of sedatives and Selective Serotonin Reuptake
Inhibitors. You moved your chair closer
to mine. My tongue tripped; I said
sorry when I meant to say *thank you.*
A button was pressed in my gut,
my eyes became, for a second,
wet. You assessed:

It's best not apologize for things you
don't need to be sorry for
nine times out of ten.

THE ROAD TO SAINTHOOD

I have just finished a semester in the southeastern townships of
Québec, so believe me when I tell you that *fragment* is an adjective
that translates roughly into English as *fragile* or *delicate*.

One is supposed to hold old photographs with covered fingers.
Cloth gloves are best, latex being allergenic to borders and matte
surfaces. Take this photograph, for instance: *Our Lady of the Lowered Lids,*
hands in her taffeta lap, that soft brown sickness, as though a sparrow
had slipped from her blanketed palms and all the other birds dove
toward its tainted human scent with their beaks cracked open.
Frenchmen refuse praise in their helpful label: *St. OCD,* or
Our Lady of Perpetual Anxiety of Borderline Features.

All this time I have been waiting—*patiently*—
for you to transform my name into a diagnosis.
Our Lady of the Lowered Lids has been recorded,
at least. The photographer paid attention
and christened her as *a possible case* of something.
She is sick in her noticing. But the physician turns
his camera toward her—and then a photo makes
this careful naming *possible*. It pays attention.
Good patients wait for such beatification.
For someone—like you—someone with two
consonants and period placed before your
Christian name to connect a specific
tremor in our fingers to our file.

S.ELECTIVE S.OOTHING R.ADIANT I.NVENTORY:
a cento drawn from the flower innards notebook

To be precise about precise about the expanse of flesh
takes the eye away from the grey words
until the self dis-owns
birds gather[ed] into the mesquite tree confessing to existence
the self. They've told
how people get over themselves. That mystery:
this life you returned to me, this one life
beyond the cruel reach
winter, an individual summer.
In the middle of the tunnel,
each moment is place,
how many of these places in space have already been
earth as full of life as life was full of them.
When next we find ourselves
don't give up the ghost. What we mean is
       attend.

MUSE IN AUGUST

Her muse for poetry is an old woman. She declares this on an island in the wilderness—it doesn't matter where as long as it's either Ontario or Québec. She says her mother was always kind to her. Her mother says she would leave her young daughter alone in the kitchen, baking. Alone with flour, eggs, oven, elements, because she didn't want to discourage her but couldn't watch her do it wrong. The Crone Muse prefers heavy, dense sentences. The Muse as Landscape says *I am the road you are walking on, pay attention.* The Muse as Pioneer Housewife hides the bodies of her sons beneath wet soil as territorial markers. Sometimes the Crone Muse says *I am happy.* She forever holds someone's memory of burnt cookies—an absence with the flavour of smoke and hard crust.

DAUGHTER CELLS

Who said this hulking, waving edifice of all
the time green is the same as that spindly
falling off running the waters in Lake Country?

Or that the warm puddle of water slow
rivering Muskoka is the same as that wild
jade thrust Skeena our father hip-waded
into as we sat disappearing on the banks of
the Copper, alone in our parallel play?

Me thinking the stones vivid as dollhouse
furniture. You, blonde and smaller, drawn
to the sand, deciduous teeth missing.
Who says this country is of one piece?

Between these wonderful monsters of
shivering conifer and the lapsing reds and
yellows, there is an empty prairie that will
teach us to be grateful for the rain and to
empathize with every tree.

The relationship between things includes
your abscission from my boreal position,
spectacular softwood of my present moment.
*The brightest leaf colours are produced when
days grow short and nights are cool but
remain above freezing.*

Our cytokinesis

Your surprising distance.

STANZA IS THE ITALIAN WORD FOR ROOM

*On benedick's retirement, or how I learned to stop worrying
and love the catholic church*

It is so holy to be old.
(Virus meas ingravecente atate non iam apte esse.)
Grandma in her white carpet stanza
refuses to install track lighting (it's tacky)
to highlight the glitter in her dying eyes.
Opa shared his final stanza with two strangers,
crippled fingers scrawling fugues on scrap paper,
unable to unfold his fingers over the keys.
Oma in her condo marvels at the SkyTrain,
popeye pizza and hoards dietary supplements
in her kitchen drawer.

Uncle Morris in the Okanagan sun stanza
still smiled when his sister-in-law whispered *chess*
into his large-lobed ear while Aunt Barbara refuses to visit,
walking with one glass eye in the empty lots in Lumby
where she said his spirit lived.

Then Uncle George just dying
in his diapers, losing his dreams
of a *Whites-only* golf course
as a swift-fingered Filapina
sponged his slack limbs.

Finally you, benedick, your shoulders
bent forward in heavy red,
a supplicant posture, just another
broken holy father.

AT LAST THE STARS: AN ORTHODOX EASTER SONNET

Some German poet, some Impressionist
drawing us at last to the word star.
Perhaps this is the year we begin to
learn how to speak of colour.
Witness this plastic keyboard accident—
Icons, emoticons: tiny asteroids
instead of primary red blood muscles.
My mis-text. Your reply: *stars 4 hearts.*
Vestiges of French immersion. Oh you.
Je t'ètoile. Everywhere wireless. This
AM radio: stars wet with shining
to please you. Impressionist face bright in
the daily falling and rising of the sun.
One of our stars, all gold. All yellow.

NOTES ON THE POEMS AND HODAYOT

"Dead Sea Scrolls: A Dissertation Erasure" and "Post-doctoral, Fellowship: The Wedding Ceremony" are repurposed from an unfinished dissertation. The work of scholars Philip Alexander, James Davila, Bilhah Nitzan, Carol Newsom, Eileen Schuller, and especially, Crispin Fletcher-Louis, informs the language a great deal. "Post-doctoral, Fellowship" is particularly interested in the document 4Q502 from the Dead Sea Scrolls. In this tattered document, the term 'the Daughter of Truth', (Hebrew בת אמת) is used once in a fragmentary context. The term is unparalleled in ancient Hebrew writing. See the discussions of M. Baillet, *Qumrân Grotte 4 III (4Q482-4Q520)*, Vol. 7, Discoveries in the Judean Desert. (Oxford: Clarendon Press, 1982); J.M. Baumgarten, "4Q502, Marriage or Golden Age Ritual." *Journal of Jewish Studies 34* (1983): 125–35 and M. Satlow, "4Q502: A New Years Ritual." *Dead Sea Discoveries 5* (1998): 57–68.

The poems in "Singular Room Occupancy: Cantos from Main and Hastings" borrow language from Dorothy Sayers' translation of Dante's Purgatorio. The second part of "Riff on Canto Six" is an erasure of that Canto.

"Elegy, a rain fragment" was inspired by a poem by Susan Steudel.

The poems "What a Queer Thing Touch Is" and "Dr. Gachet's Walk" are inspired by the letters of Vincent van Gogh and the Gospels of John & Mark.

The lines in the Cento are drawn from books of poetry I read in the early part of 2013 and recorded in an "Art of Instruction" notebook. The line order was determined sequentially from the order in which my fingers divined them (eyes closed, random flipping and pointing). The lines are: P.K. Page, "Winter Afternoon" (the doubling of "precise about" was a slip of pen and is not found in Page's original); Ted Berrigan, "Sonnet LIX"; Jen Currin, "The Bridge Melting Behind Us"; Alice Notley, "Language of Mercy" (I have changed the original "gather" into "gather[ed]" for the purposes of tense comprehension); Jan Zwicky, "Art of Fugue"; Anne Carson, "Aeroplane" (this line impressed itself incorrectly on me and I recorded it incorrectly. The original line is "How people get power over one another, / this mystery." I am uncertain why I skipped over "power"); Evelyn Lau, "Quayside"; Robert Priest, "Noah's Dark"; Albert Camus, "The Myth of Sisyphus" (I have accidentally transcribed "individual" instead of "indivisible"); Denise Levertov, "Part III; ix"; Mark Strand, "Black Maps"; Rainier Maria Rilke, "Second Part; I" from *Sonnets to Orpheus*. (the original German is "Wie viele von diesen Stellen der Räume waren schon"); Frank O'Hara, "A Step Away from Them"; Carole Glasser Langille, "A Letter"; Patricia Young, "Heartsick"; Phyllis Webb, " 'Attend' ".

Poems in this collection were previously published in *CV2, Prairie Fire, The Malahat Review, PRISM*, the *Literary Review of Canada*, and *Dreamland*. "My Psychiatrist Was a Math Major" won Editor's Choice in Arc's Poem of the Year Contest, and I thank Lise Rochefort for her generous reading of the poem. The van Gogh poems appeared in my chapbook *The whole and broken yellows*. Thanks to Shane Neilson.

One of the lines from the Hodayot (the Dead Sea Thanksgiving Psalms) is "I thank you Lord because you rescued my life from the pit." It's a bit dramatic, but I would like to extend that kind of gratitude to Shannon Maguire, Barbara Baydala, Chelene Knight, Matea Kulić, Leena Niemela, Cary O'Malley, Natasha Barber, Barbro Koch (all daughters of truth), Jeremy Penner, Garth Kroeker, Gwen Bevan, Eva Mroczek, Kerry Shawn Keyes, Allison Brown, Ryan Jones, Rebekka Regan, Jennifer Lapierre, Marian Brown and, especially, Jen Currin. Also, of course, to Jay and Hazel at BookThug.

JENNIFER ZILM is a Vancouver-based poet. She is a graduate of The Writer's Studio at Simon Fraser University and the Humber School for Writers, and has a master's degree in biblical studies from the University of British Columbia. Zilm's writing has been published in numerous journals, including *PRISM International, Prairie Fire, Grain, CV2, The Antigonish Review, Vallum,* and *Women in Judaism and Poetry.* Zilm is the author of two chapbooks: *The whole and broken yellows* (2013) and *October Notebook* (2015). Zilm has been a finalist for many contests, including *The Malahat Review*'s Far Horizons Award and *CV2*'s 2-Day Poem Contest. A draft of *Waiting Room* was shortlisted for the 2014 Robert Kroetsch Award for Innovative Poetry.

COLOPHON

Manufactured as the first edition of *Waiting Room* in the spring of 2016 by BookThug. Distributed in Canada by the Literary Press Group: www.lpg.ca. Distributed in the US by Small Press Distribution: www.spdbooks.org.

Shop online at www.bookthug.ca.

BOOK
PRODUCTION
WAR ECONOMY
STANDARD

Cover design by Kate Hargreaves
Text by Jay MillAr
Copy edited by Ruth Zuchter